Escapes or Renew: Can Traveling do Both?

Travel's Role in Mental Wellness, Happiness, and Self-Discovery

Elizabeth Delgado

Copyright © 2023 by Elizabeth Delgado

Visit the author's website at www.rainbowtextpublishing.com

All rights reserved.

No portion of this book may be reproduced in any form without written permission from the publisher or author, except as permitted by U.S. copyright law.

This publication is designed to provide accurate and authoritative information in regard to the subject matter covered. It is sold with the understanding that neither the author nor the publisher is engaged in rendering legal, investment, accounting, or other professional services. While the publisher and author have used their best efforts in preparing this book, they make no representations or warranties with respect to the accuracy or completeness of the contents of this book and specifically disclaim any implied warranties of merchantability or fitness for a particular purpose. No warranty may be created or extended by sales representatives or written sales materials. The author is not a health professional and the insights shared in this book are based on personal experiences and observations. The advice and strategies contained herein may not be suitable for your situation. You should consult with a professional when appropriate. Neither the publisher nor the author shall be liable for any loss of profit or any other commercial damages, including but not limited to special, incidental, consequential, personal, or other damages.

Disclaimer:

The information contained in this book is for general information purposes only. The author and publisher have made every effort to ensure the accuracy and completeness of the information contained herein. However, they make no warranties, expressed or implied, regarding the accuracy, completeness, reliability, or suitability of this information. The author and publisher shall not be held liable for any loss or damage arising from or in connection with the use of, or reliance upon, any information provided in this book.

The opinions expressed in this book are those of the author alone and do not reflect the views of the publisher or any other organization. Travel conditions, laws, and regulations may change over time. It is the responsibility of the reader to check the current conditions and legal requirements before embarking on any travel. The inclusion of third-party information, links, or references does not imply endorsement by the author or publisher.

For rights and permissions, please contact:

Elizabeth Delgado

PO Box 1478

New York, NY 10163

liz@rainbowtextpublishing.com

www.RainbowTextPublishing.com

Contents

Introduction	X
Exposing Travel Myths	1
1. Cost of Travel	3

Airlines: Navigating the Skies and Your Wallet

Hotel Accommodations: Selecting the Perfect Stay for Your Travel Needs

Transportation: Understanding your Transportation Options Abroad

Savoring the Local Cuisine: An Exploration of Taste

Exploring Beyond the Hotel: Sightseeing and Activities

The Art of Selecting Souvenirs: Preserving Memories Without Breaking the Bank

2. Finding Time to Travel	15

Strategizing Work Leaves: Stretching Your Vacation Days to the Max

Maximizing Shorter Trips: Frequent Escapes over One Long Getaway

Embracing Flexibility: The New Norm of Remote Work and Workcations

Mapping Out Your Travels: The Importance of Setting Travel Goals

Prioritizing Travel: A Promise to Personal Growth

Planning Your Travels Early: Setting the Stage for Your Adventure

3. Navigating Language Differences	22

4.	Safety Concerns	24
5.	Charting Family Voyages	26
6.	Defining Travel Age	28

The Rewards of Traveling   31

7. Mental Health   33
> Travel's Effects on Stress Relief
> Enhances Creativity
> Builds Resilience & Mental Agility
> Self-Discovery and Personal Growth
> Boosting Mental Focus and Productivity Through Exploration
> Enhancing Emotional Health: The Power of Travel

8. Fortifying the Body   39

9. Living in the Moment   41

10. Embarking on a Journey of Self-Discovery   43
> Cultural Awareness
> Empathy and Compassion
> Adaptability
> Confidence
> Communication Skills
> Self-Discovery

11. Traveling Together   49
> Creating Memories Together
> Quality Time
> Communication and Teamwork
> Shared Interests
> Building Trust
> Rekindles Romance

12. Embracing the World   53
> Celebrating Differences
> Promoting Peace Through Understanding

13. Exploring Career Paths Through Travel   54

    Networking

    Language Skills

    Inspiration and Creativity

    Business Opportunities

    Market Research

    Building your Personal Brand

Final Thoughts   58

Join Our Exclusive Travel Community!   60

New Book Coming Soon!   62

Wander More, Worry Less: 63

About the Author   65

Join Our Exclusive Travel Community!

Embark on a Journey with Our Exclusive Travel Community!

Are you ready to elevate your travel experiences? I warmly invite you to join our Travel Readers Club, an exclusive community for those who share a passion for exploration and discovery. As a member, you'll unlock a world of invaluable resources designed to enhance every aspect of your journey.

Imagine having access to the best discounts on airfare and hotels, making your dream destinations more attainable than ever. We'll also provide you with comprehensive packing lists tailored for every season and destination - be it a winter wonderland, a summer beach escape, European adventures, or luxurious cruises.

But that's not all! You'll also discover a suite of essential apps and websites, meticulously curated to help you organize your itineraries, breeze through airport security, and stay informed and safe wherever your travels take you.

Join our Travel Readers Club today and transform the way you travel, making each trip more efficient, enjoyable, and extraordinary. Once you sign up, you will receive a link where you can download the documents containing the above travel resources, and stay updated on new book releases.

Sign up here https://www.rainbowtextpublishing.com/travel-readers-group

All icons are clickable

AIRFARE
Websites/Apps where you can find cheap airfare

TRAVEL APPS

RESOURCES
Resources to help make your travel easier, faster and safe

HOTEL DISCOUNT MEMBERSHIPS
Discounts in airfare and hotels through a membership

If you need help planning that long-awaited adventure, feel free to visit my Travel Agency's, Never Stop Packing Travel, at our website www.NeverStopPacking.com

Introduction

I can still remember the excitement I felt on my first international flight—to Italy. My mind was full of images of famous landmarks that I had only seen in movies and through social media. I tried preparing for this trip by learning a few basic phrases: 'Buongiorno', 'Buonasera', and 'Grazie'. These basic words were my safeguard, all I would use to navigate this unfamiliar country. This was my gesture of respect for this new culture.

A rush of exhilaration washed over me, besides a hint of anxiety. I was about to dive into a country full of ancient history, equipped with nothing but a handful of phrases and my wits. There were no local guides, no friends to help me out, no safety nets.

I was about to navigate an unknown language, an unfamiliar transportation system, and the absolute unpredictability that comes with traveling. But none of these things bothered me enough to stop me from taking on this journey. Anticipation and excitement filled me as I thought about the impending adventure.

My most vivid memory of that trip wasn't the incredible visit to the Colosseum, where Roman gladiators fought hundreds of years ago, or the jaw-opening beauty of St. Peter's Basilica. It was my visit to a charming little restaurant in the center of Rome, near the Trevi Fountain. It was there that my husband and I struck a conversation with our server. Though we could notice her exhaustion from the day's work, she was kind enough to gift us a smile and engage us in small talk.

At that moment, we faced the challenge of our lifetime. We pieced together a conversation with our very limited Italian and her broken English, with a dash of Spanish. Amidst the struggle, we connected.

We exchanged clips about or everyday lives and challenges, as she shared she was at retirement age and still needed to work to sustain herself. We understood her struggle and sympathized with her situation.

It was a humble and deep interaction that transcended language barriers. I walked away from that restaurant feeling thrilled, accomplished and very proud of myself. Never would I've thought I'd be able to have that type of conversation with a local in a country I've never visited.

This, I thought, is what traveling is about. We travel to have fun, of course. But it shouldn't be our only reason to travel. We need to connect with other cultures, understand their lifestyle and sympathize with everyone's struggles.

The world is too large and doesn't revolve around a single person, culture, or country. It is vast, diverse, and full of learning experiences that will make you a better person if you allow it.

Saint Augustine once said, "The world is a book and those who do not travel read only one page." Oh, how true that is! After my first travel adventure, I decided that there was too much out there to see. I promised myself I would do all in my power to see the world. Going along with Saint Augustine's words, I refuse to read only one page of this amazing book called world.

Traveling is more than just taking selfies in beautiful places or sharing every step you take on social media; it's a learning experience. It helps us become more adaptable, encourages us to step out of our comfort zones, and develop a unique independence within us. An independence many of us never knew we could achieve.

I also connect with another saying, which goes, "Travel is the only thing you buy that makes you richer." This saying is also dear to my heart. The richness that traveling brings isn't in physical items, but a wealth of experiences and long-lasting memories — the kind you can't put a price on and will cherish for years to come.

In this book, we're going on an exciting journey to understand travel's life-changing effects. We'll explore the many advantages it introduces to our lives, from improving mental well-being and reducing stress to encouraging personal development and breaking down mental obstacles.

Our goal is to tackle common misconceptions that prevent people from traveling, challenging the idea that it's always costly, risky, or too much to handle. Our approach involves navigating challenges by providing practical strategies for turning common pretexts into justifications. Clearing the path toward your goal, to see the world and all its beautiful diversity.

Before we begin our journey, here's a little about me. I'm more than just your guide; I am a travel enthusiast who is passionate about the world's diverse cultures, breathtaking landscapes, and hidden treasures. My love for exploration has led me to various places, from lively, crowded cities to tranquil spots far from the usual tourist trails.

These personal journeys have not only brought fulfillment and happiness to my life, but have also sparked a desire to spread the joy of traveling to others.

This love for travel led me to start a home-based travel agency. You may ask yourself, 'A travel agency nowadays?' Yes. My passion is too great to keep it to myself, so I share it the best way I can. By helping others make their travel dreams come true. And now my latest endeavor, sharing my passions through written words.

Every day, I get to create memorable experiences for my clients, customizing trips to match their desires and dreams, helping them handle their fears, and rejoicing in the incredible stories they return with.

This book continues that passion—it's a collection of knowledge gained from years of my own travels and professional know-how, aimed at motivating, navigating, and helping you as you consider your future travels adventures.

So, I invite you: get ready and leave any preconceived notions at the door as we embark on this enlightening journey together. We'll learn that travel is not just about having fun or visiting the most famous landmarks.

We'll discover that travel offers us benefits that money can't buy, such as mental wellness, personal growth, and something as simple as pure joy. It's more than just learning how to travel; it is about welcoming a life enriched by our adventures.

Exposing Travel Myths

Bringing Down the Barriers to Your Dream Adventures

In our vast and diverse world, it's quite common for misunderstandings about travel to invade the minds of those who are thinking of venturing out. These misconceptions, often formed from partial truths and exaggerated worries, can suppress the urge to explore and create unseen obstacles to extraordinary adventures.

In the following chapters, we're going to reveal the truth behind some widespread travel misconceptions. We'll guide you through common errors when thinking about expenses, safety, language challenges, and more, lighting the way with facts and personal experiences.

Our goal in addressing these myths is to clear any doubts, broaden your horizons, inspire you to step beyond familiar surroundings and into a journey of worldwide exploration.

Now, let's tackle these travel myths, eliminating any doubts or confusions that may prevent you from setting out on your next adventure. We'll dismantle these misconceptions one at a time, making sure they don't obstruct your travel aspirations.

And once we've cleared the way, we'll move to the most rewarding part of this book - uncovering the deep, transformative BENEFITS of travel. Prepare to discover not just how to travel, but how each journey can deeply enhance your life in ways you never expected.

A Journey Through Time and Economics

Travel, half a century ago, was a unique experience from the extensive choices available to us today. In the 1970s, flying was not an everyday activity. It was a luxury, characterized by fewer flight choices and destinations, all wrapped in an appearance of allure and privilege. Only those with the financial means could travel, leaving the rest with just dreams of traveling.

Dive to the present, and the change is nothing less than extraordinary. A surge in competition among airlines, hotels, and other travel services has rewritten the rules, driving prices down and bringing the once-distant dream of traveling within reach for most.

Now, let's ease your concerns about costs and show you how to manage these expenses by shedding some light on some of the key figures in the travel sector, which encompass your travel budget.

CHAPTER 1

Cost of Travel

Budgeting, Saving, and Maximizing Your Travel Dollars

Airlines: Navigating the Skies and Your Wallet

There's a common belief that air travel is a costly luxury, too great a financial investment for some individuals and unachievable for a whole family. It's no secret that flight costs have increased tenfold in the last several decades and diminished the high service quality they once provided.

Unfortunately, airfare is the most expensive component of traveling and can take up a sizeable portion of your travel funds. But there are ways to cut down this substantial cost, although it requires careful thought and planning. Now, let's discuss some ways we can discourage the notion that airfare is too expensive for you to travel.

This is where budget airlines come in, serving as both a blessing and a curse. They are lifesavers for those on a strict budget, offering the possibility of travel without breaking the bank. But you need to be aware: the upfront fare price is just the beginning of other charges to come.

These budget or economy airlines recover their losses from discounted fares by charging a set of extra fees such as paying for your carry-on luggage, a comfortable seat, even a soft drink might have a price tag, depending on the airline.

Your cheap ticket could multiply into a much more expensive one, due to all these fees, hence defeating the purpose of saving money.

So, what should you do? It boils down to attention to detail and basic math. Before you get drawn by a low airfare, consider the additional costs for the essentials you'll need, or want, during your flight.

Check how this total measures up against prices from other premium airlines, which may include more amenities in their standard fare. Some of these included amenities could be a carry-on luggage, checked luggage, refundable/changeable fare, and free seat selection.

When choosing an airline ticket, think about how long your flight will be. For long flights, paying a bit more for comfort and convenience is justified, especially when the final prices aren't so far apart from the budget airline fares.

Another smart way to cut costs is to book your tickets well in advance. Waiting to book until the last minute will cost you more, most of the time.

If you have some flexibility with your travel dates, try not to fly during busy periods like major holidays — think 4th of July, Labor Day, Thanksgiving, and Christmas. It's tougher to find good deals during these dates, unless you book with at least six months of anticipation.

Another good way to save on airfare is traveling during off-peak seasons. Fares tend to go up during summer, when kids are out of school, and during other major school break times like spring and Christmas. If you are traveling with children during their school break, your saving options may reduce dramatically.

Choosing to travel in quieter, less sought-after dates can save you money and give you a more peaceful, genuine experience. Allowing you the opportunity to enjoy your sights and attractions without the endless lines, masses of people, and expensive accommodations.

These are a few of many ways you can make booking airfare more manageable and affordable. Helping you head out to your next travel adventure.

Hotel Accommodations: Selecting the Perfect Stay for Your Travel Needs

To explore the range of hotel options available can be overwhelming, especially when you're trying to be mindful of your budget. The cost of accommodations depends on various factors, the first being location.

The following conditions will also increase the price of accommodations: staying at a hotel in prime location or near a tourist hub. A hotel that offers a variety of amenities, such as a gym, spa services, and concierge service. Let's not forget the hotel's category or rating. Staying at a 5-star hotel or a luxury name brand hotel will also increase your nightly rate.

There are plenty of accommodation options for all budgets and tastes. It's just a matter of choosing what's most important for you: location, amenities, or staying within your budget.

My accommodation requirements are easy, the property must be clean, have basic hotel services, near public transportation, and very important, it must be in a safe area. Once a hotel fulfills these requirements, I'll stay wherever fits my budget. Now, let's discuss the different accommodations available.

Diverse Choices for Every Budget

Travel accommodations come in all forms, providing options for the low budget to the luxury traveler. Let's begin with the options available for those who are on a budget.

Hostels are a very affordable option, but they have a downside. They offer shared rooms, which you share with at least 2 guests or more. Some hostels can offer rooms that hold up to 8 guests, and others can offer private rooms, but at a higher price. You lack privacy, risk having your belongings stolen (they offer bins for this purpose).

Another downside, you must share a bathroom, and receive very limited amenities, if any. This is a very popular option among young travelers, especially backpackers traveling across Europe. It is a great option if you want to socialize and meet new people from across the globe and not break the bank while you're at it.

When looking for a bit more comfort without excessive spending, standard hotel chains and small boutique hotels are available. These offer basic hotel amenities and customer service, all within reasonable price ranges. Prices will vary depending on the hotel chain you select.

An excellent option is all-inclusive resorts, which include your stay and all meals, plus drinks, for a flat rate, saving you lots of money in food and drinks. These resorts provide a great number of amenities, all under the same price tag.

This all-inclusive option allows you to focus on enjoying your stay, instead of worrying about your final hotel bill at check-out time. You can find from basic to luxury all-inclusive resorts, allowing you to choose based on your budget and taste. This is my favorite accommodation type when I visit Mexico or the Caribbean.

If you want to indulge yourself, then high-end resorts and luxury hotels offer top-notch services and amenities. These properties are in prime locations and will cater to your every whim. Of course, there will be a price to pay for this type of accommodation, and it won't be a small one.

Vacation Rentals

If you want to stay somewhere you can enjoy that home feeling you love, especially if you're traveling with a large group or family, then vacation rentals are a great choice.

You can rent full houses or apartments, for any time period and with all the comforts of a home, depending on the property. You can find basic to luxury vacation properties available for rent in many locations around the globe.

Rental service platforms, such as Airbnb and Vrbo, are great options for vacation rentals. However, these rentals might not have the same level of service and amenities you'd find in a hotel. For example, there will not be a reception desk available to offer guidance or a concierge to help you with specific needs.

It's important to know that the prices for these vacation rentals have gone up in recent years. You can find properties costing as much as, or sometimes a lot more, than a hotel offering full services and amenities.

So, if staying within a preset budget is important to you, I suggest you compare prices between vacation rentals and hotels to see which is more convenient for you and stays within your budget limit.

Smart Booking Strategies

Regardless of where you choose to stay, you can save money by using a few smart booking tactics. You can begin by making your reservation far in advance. The farther from your travel date, the better. When you book too close to your check-in date, you risk paying a higher-than-usual fare.

Hotels sometimes offer last-minute promotions or discounts to fill up their rooms when they have too many vacancies. You may get lucky and book a discounted fare, but there is no guarantee and way of knowing until you book. This is a chance I will never take if I'm traveling on a budget.

Another way to save is by checking into the hotel early in the week, let's say, between Monday and Wednesday, depending on the location of the hotel. If the hotel caters to tourists, checking in early or mid-week is your best bet to get a better rate. City hotels that cater to business travelers may offer a better rate when checking in during the weekend.

This is not a rule set in stone and it may vary by hotel. Another factor that can change this rule is if there are any special events or conferences in the surrounding area. If there are any events in the area, prices will be more expensive than usual and there will be less availability.

In summary, reserve your spot early, check in early or mid-week, and choose accommodations away from popular areas or tourist centers to help reduce costs. It's essential to balance cost-saving with convenience.

In the end, the best place to stay is one that suits your financial comfort, personal preferences, and travel aspirations. Whether it's the reliability of a hotel or the cozy feel of a home-style rental, making an informed decision can make your trip enjoyable without costing you too much.

Transportation: Understanding your Transportation Options Abroad

Arranging and budgeting for transportation is key when piecing together your vacation. Your decisions will depend on several factors, including where you will travel to, how convenient transportation is at the destination, what it costs, and what method of transportation you prefer to use while visiting.

The below methods of transportation are more targeted towards travel in Europe, but they can also be practical to travel within the United States. Let's explore these options:

Taxis & Ride-Share Services

Taxis and ride-share services are great for getting you right where you want to go without the hassles of making unnecessary stops, but they might cost more than public transportation. In addition, chatting with local drivers can be very helpful and full of useful information that can help improve your travel experience.

When taking a taxi while traveling abroad, it's important you choose a licensed taxi driver. A lot of unlicensed drivers offer taxi services, which could be a problem if you were to get into a car accident or have any incident with the driver.

By being unlicensed, the driver will not be insured and in case of an accident, you cannot submit any claims.

Since they are not regulated, this allows them to increase your fare as they please, particularly if they recognize you as a tourist. Always go to a taxi stand, and if you're going to hail one, make sure it's identified as a taxi.

Ride-share services are a great option to choose if there's availability in the city you're visiting. Uber is well known across the United States, and it's available in several European cities.

Most large cities across Europe have their own ride-share apps, which is another option you can use during your travels. These local apps may prove to be cheaper than Uber.

I recommend you download the local rideshare app so you can compare prices against those offered by Uber. This will allow you to book the one that offers the cheapest ride. I prefer ride-share services since it allows me to know where I'm going, and how much my ride will cost me. Avoiding unpleasant surprises at the end of my ride.

Car Rental

I recommend renting a car if you're visiting a location where public transport isn't accessible; it doesn't provide great service, or if you like the freedom to come and go as you please. Don't forget to add the extra expenses of renting a car, such as insurance, gas, tolls, parking, and other fees the rental companies might include in your rental.

The perk of renting a car? You get to discover hidden places on your own schedule. When you rent a car, you can go where you want, near or far, and take as long as you need. Unlike taking public transportation to a location farther away, where you need to be mindful of the transportation schedules to make sure you do not miss your last transport back to your accommodations.

Another situation: when you go on a tour and you have a tight schedule, sometimes leaves you wishing you'd spent more time at your favorite spots visited. Renting a car will eliminate the need to worry about not spending enough time at your favorite spots. These are all valid reasons to justify renting a car.

Buses / Trains

Choosing public transportation, especially for transferring between major cities, can save you a lot of money. It's a dependable (most of the time), and a low-cost option, plus it gives you a real taste of what the local life is like, making your experience more authentic.

Public buses are a great option since they allow you to see the landscape of a new city while en route to your destination.

The downside is that you can experience a lot of traffic, depending on the city, which may rob you of precious time you can use doing other activities.

Another downside is that they may not be as punctual as the metro or rails. You may spend hours waiting for a bus, making it ineffective time wise.

Taking the metro is a great option. They are fast, economical, and on time. Many metro systems offer ticket bundles which are an excellent way to save money if you will use it often during your stay. Metros are an excellent way to get a sense of how the locals commute daily.

Also, taking high-speed trains between European cities is an excellent option. Although high-speed trains may take longer than a flight, they are reasonably priced and allow you to see the scenery while en route. This is my favorite method of transportation, after walking, when visiting a European city.

Walking / Bike Rental

For experiencing a new destination, especially those walkable city centers in Europe, nothing beats going by foot or bike. It's a fantastic way to stay active, and it also gives you a unique perspective on the local culture, people, and landmarks.

If you're planning on walking to the attractions you want to visit, plan ahead of time and coordinate your visits by area. I recommend you go to Google Maps, or your favorite maps application, and pin all the attractions you want to visit. Group them by area, ensuring they are within walking distance, one from the other.

This will save you some money on transportation and keep you active during your travels, allowing you to enjoy the local delicacies without worrying about gaining weight.

Of course, there will be times where you'll have to take a taxi or public transportation, but if you plan correctly, you should be able to keep these to the minimum.

As for renting a bike in European cities, I recommend you ride carefully if you rent one. Please do some research on how the locals drive before renting a bike. This will allow you to know if you'll be able to handle biking around local drivers.

You'd be surprised at the driving etiquette of certain European cities. It may feel you hold your life in your hands every time you cross a street. This is so in the city of Naples, Italy.

Trying to figure out all your transportation options needn't be overwhelming. With some strategic planning, you can make the most of your travel budget without missing out on the experiences and sacrificing the richness of your journey.

Whether you're enjoying the ease of a taxi, the freedom of a rental car, the down-to-earth feel of public transportation, or the intimacy of walking or biking, each has its own benefits and perks.

The secret is to pick what suits your travel preferences, budget, and love for adventure. Remember, how you travel is as important as where you're going and making smart transportation choices can elevate your travel experience from ordinary to extraordinary.

Savoring the Local Cuisine: An Exploration of Taste

To experience local cuisine is a fundamental part of any vacation. This means that you will dive into the food culture of wherever you are. Part of the attraction of visiting a new country is to taste its local cuisine.

Enjoying the local cuisine doesn't have to drain your wallet, though it can if first-class, Michelin-starred cuisine is your heart's desire. But for those who enjoy discovering authentic local eats, savoring street food, or stumbling upon a cute café, you can indulge without breaking the bank.

As travelers, we often become food adventurers, eager to try new dishes, even if we struggle to pronounce them. If you want to have an authentic food experience, and not overpay, avoid the restaurants that target tourists. They are known for their uninspiring, many times bland, and overpriced dishes.

These spots are common, especially around well-known tourist areas in European cities, recognizable by their extensive photo menus, translated in many languages, and over-enthusiastic hosts calling you in to visit their restaurant.

I learned this the hard way at a Rome restaurant overlooking the Trevi Fountain. This visit resulted in a large bill, compared to New York City prices, for a very unremarkable dinner, one I could've prepared myself at home.

Exploring the local culinary landscape isn't just about spending less; it's a dive into the cultural heart of the places you visit. You can find the real essence of a region's cuisine in its busy food markets, simple street vendors, and small, family-run restaurants.

These places often represent the heart of a city's culinary world. In the smaller restaurants you will find better food quality, better prices, and a more authentic experience, compared to the high-traffic tourist spots.

Therefore, when drafting your travel budget, recognize that food represents more than just having a meal; it's an immersive experience. Budget carefully, venture outside tourist hotspots, and embrace the unexpected culinary treasures you will encounter.

The tales you'll share won't focus on the expenses incurred, but on the memories created and the authentic tastes that added life to your travels.

Exploring Beyond the Hotel: Sightseeing and Activities

Travel is more than staying within the pleasant boundaries of your hotel. It's about immersing yourself in your destination and experiencing the renowned wonders that have the world talking. However, these adventures can become expensive with admission charges to your favorite attractions.

Here's a helpful tip: many cities in the U.S. and Europe provide 'City Passes,' which allow entry to many major attractions for one flat price. If your visit is short or focused on visiting a handful of attractions, a pass may not be the most economical choice. However, for those wishing to experience an entire city's highlights, or as many as you can, this option could save you a lot of money.

Here's how to plan: calculate the total of the entry fees for the attractions you want to visit. If a city pass offers access to these for less, it's a clear win.

Take into consideration the number of museums that offer free admission, especially on certain days of the week or for specific demographic groups (like seniors, students, etc.). A little research in advance can lead to notable savings during your trip.

Don't miss out on the enriching experiences that cost nothing. Just because it's free doesn't mean the experience will be mediocre. For example, free walking tours conducted by knowledgeable locals offer a deep dive into the city's history and secret spots.

While there's no set fee for these tours, it's good manners (and well appreciated) to tip your guide in cash. Remember to use local currency when tipping.

Platforms like Viator or Get Your Guide, as well as official country /city tourism sites, are excellent resources for finding these unique walking tours. Don't forget to add local parks, spur-of-the-moment street shows, local markets, and lively festivals in your plans. These experiences provide a glimpse of everyday culture without straining your budget.

To set aside money for sightseeing is crucial; it forms the core of your travel experience. Not allocating enough funds for this aspect can lead to a feeling of having missed out, leaving you longing for what could have been a more vivid, profound memory of your trip.

By planning wisely, your journey can go beyond typical tourism, becoming a memorable discovery of unknown places.

The Art of Selecting Souvenirs: Preserving Memories Without Breaking the Bank

Another component of travel expenses often comes as souvenirs, an area of spending that can skyrocket if not kept under control. It's normal to want a physical memento from our travels, an item that represents the essence of our travel experiences.

However, the proper task is to avoid the trap of overspending on trinkets that become more about clutter than cherished memories.

Truth be told, there's a limit to the number of keychains one can own and find useful. These items, while popular, often lose their appeal with each subsequent purchase. It might be more prudent to consider souvenirs that are useful.

For instance, I love gifting t-shirts since they serve a practical purpose, and everyone finds use for a t-shirt. You can find these at reasonable prices in local markets or city stores, unlike their overpriced counterparts in airport shops.

However, not all keepsakes come at a cost. An affectionate and modern twist could be to create a digital photo album. Gather the standout moments, the spontaneous snapshots, the breathtaking vistas, and turn them into a digital story to share with friends and family.

This method captures memories in a format that's accessible and you can revisit at any moment. The best part, it won't cost you a penny, just a little of your time.

But, if you prefer physical souvenirs, perhaps because of a family tradition or the pleasure of gifting, it's wise to allocate a part of your budget for these purchases. This is simple, thoughtful planning helps keep your overall travel expenses under control, protecting your overall travel experience.

CHAPTER 2

Finding Time to Travel

Making Space for the World in Your Busy Schedule

In our modern, fast-paced work culture, especially within dynamic cities, finding time for travel—even with available paid leave—seems like an unreachable luxury. Maybe we are involved in too many personal projects, or it's just not the right time to travel. If we think about it, there will always be something stopping us from traveling.

However, the deep desire to discover unknown places calls us to put our excuses aside and manage our time smartly to take that well-deserved break.

The good news is, there are several effective ways to ensure we can enjoy the vacation time we've earned and yearn. In this chapter, we'll explore useful advice and perspectives to balance work responsibilities and personal engagements, setting the stage for your impending exciting journey.

Strategizing Work Leaves: Stretching Your Vacation Days to the Max

For many working individuals, especially those navigating the corporate world, annual leave is precious. Given most of us have an average of 15 days of personal leave available each year, making the most of every single day is crucial for travel enthusiasts.

One of the cleverest tactics to maximize your holiday period involves synchronizing your days off with established company holidays.

Imagine a regular Monday-to-Friday work structure, with a public holiday falling on a Monday, presenting you with a three-day weekend. By taking off the adjacent Thursday and Friday, or perhaps the following Tuesday and Wednesday, you craft a lengthy five-day break while using only two days of your official leave.

This approach is ideal for shorter getaways or mini vacations, as I call them, allowing you the freedom to travel without impacting your accumulated vacation days.

Indeed, the strategy of aligning your vacation with public holidays has its drawbacks. Holidays are peak times for travel in the U.S., with a notable surge in both airfare and accommodation prices.

Herein lies a decision: opt for saving vacation days by leveraging public holidays, albeit with higher costs, or save money by choosing less popular travel times, which will consume more of your leave. There is no wrong choice.

This situation calls for a careful approach and consideration of what's most important to you. Consider your priorities: is it extending your vacation time, maintaining a budget, or perhaps balancing the two?

The strategic allocation of your vacation days can lead to more opportunities for exploration, each journey adding invaluable layers to your life's experiences, far beyond what money can buy.

Maximizing Shorter Trips: Frequent Escapes over One Long Getaway

The strategy of taking several shorter breaks throughout the year has changed my approach to rest and relaxation. In our fast-moving world, holding out for only one annual break can seem almost counterproductive in beating exhaustion.

I've discovered that spreading multiple shorter getaways across the year serves as the ideal solution, offering regular intervals of refreshment.

Naturally, there's a trade-off; shorter escapades don't offer the deep immersion that a prolonged stay might. It's common to feel that you're only scratching the surface of what a place offers before it's time to pack up and leave.

However, rather than seeing this as a drawback, I view it as an opportunity: it's a reason to revisit, a motive for deeper exploration, and a recurrent incentive to engage with the endless wonders around us. Each quick getaway acts as an enticing preview, a promise of the abundant travel possibilities ahead.

Whether your preference is to merge your paid time off into one extensive holiday or to fragment it into several smaller breaks, there is no right or wrong approach. The crucial aspect is allowing yourself that break—however brief—to recharge. It's about quality over quantity, soaking in each experience, and returning home renewed, one brief trip at a time.

Embracing Flexibility: The New Norm of Remote Work and Workcations

In the world of modern careers, remote work and workcations are at the forefront of offering flexibility, paving the way for a more balanced approach to our professional and personal lives.

During the COVID-19 pandemic, the corporate world had to rethink a way to carry on with business as usual, amidst all the chaos. It was during these dark times that corporate workers, and employers, discovered that they can still do the job without being present at the office.

Remote work allowed people to learn what a balanced work-life is. It proved that fulfilling your duties as an employee, while having enough time left to enjoy your home life and family was possible. This became the new work style, a priceless gift that many to this day cherish and enjoy. Let's explore these two modern concepts:

Remote Work: Your Office, Anywhere

Remote work liberates you from the confines of the traditional office, empowering you to fulfill your professional responsibilities from your home, a local coffee shop, or even a serene beach somewhere on a tropical island.

This approach requires a committed routine to maintain your professional duties, but the benefits are significant and outweigh any commitment. Imagine avoiding the rush-hour traffic, cutting down on commuting time and costs, and, of course, enjoying those additional minutes of rest in the morning.

The perks of remote work extend beyond these immediate comforts; it's a passport to global experiences. Think of it like this: once your workday concludes, you are free to go out and explore new cultures, cuisines, and experiences, enriching your global perspective.

From spending your evenings at local hangouts to crafting weekend getaways to nearby cities, your opportunities expand considerably. Have you ever imagined finishing your workday and then exploring the ancient streets of Rome or heading to a nice Caribbean beach? Remote work turns such daydreams into genuine possibilities.

Workcations: Blending Business with Pleasure

Workcations offer a unique twist on professional flexibility. Picture this: you're on a business trip, busy with meetings and work obligations. But after the job is done, instead of flying back home, you extend your visit for some personal downtime.

This extra time doesn't allow for an exhaustive exploration of the location. It serves as a delightful preview, enough to stir your appetite for a longer holiday ahead. Yes, it's a brief break, but it's an effective strategy to join work travel with personal discovery, allowing sneak peeks into different locales. An added perk of workcations is that they can cut down your airfare and accommodation costs.

Naturally, the shift towards remote work or workcations relies on your company's adaptability. It's worth starting the conversation; you never know how a simple inquiry might unfold into an opportunity, further blurring the lines between living and earning, between exploring and settling. Between working to live, rather than living to work.

Mapping Out Your Travels: The Importance of Setting Travel Goals

Amid our busy routines, the idea of travel often lingers as a distant wish, pushed aside by other pressing responsibilities. Some of these responsibilities could be a heavy work schedule, family situations, or even childcare availability. Yet, for those touched by the call of wanderlust, it's essential to turn these yearnings into clear travel objectives.

This process goes beyond just pinning far-off places on a map; it's about integrating travel into your life goals, opening doors to new cultural experiences, culinary delights, and expanded worldviews.

The act of imagining your trip is a key step toward making it happen. As you dive into the planning phase, every detail - from seeking lesser-known spots to looking forward to food explorations - serves as a source of inspiration. This approach nurtures your commitment, transforming vague dreams into solid agendas and, eventually, a reality.

Begin with some self-reflection: What draws your interest? Is it the peaceful scenery of New Zealand, the deep historical layers of Rome, or the energetic pace of Tokyo? It's simple. Where do you want to go next? Let these fascinations steer your decisions and guide you towards your next adventure.

Now, it's time to switch to planning mode. Assess the logistics, including budget, timing, and accommodations. Be realistic in your planning — consider your financial boundaries and time constraints to mold a trip that satisfies your wanderlust without straining your resources.

With your destination in mind, delve into the details. What sights are a must-see? What local experiences are essential for you? How are you going to get around? To align these elements with your passions turns anticipation into a thrilling escape from the daily grind.

Understand, setting travel goals isn't just fanciful thinking. It's a pledge to yourself to step beyond the usual and embrace the remarkable. And when your route is clear, and your arrangements are drawn up, what remains is the thrilling unfolding of experiences you've organized.

Welcome the planning phase wholeheartedly. The happiness it brings is just the beginning of a series of enriching experiences on the horizon, making every obstacle along the way worthwhile and worth the expense.

Prioritizing Travel: A Promise to Personal Growth

In our modern, busy lives, valuing travel means more than just scheduling vacation times; it involves acknowledging travel as an essential, enriching personal investment. Life, with its endless responsibilities and unforeseen challenges, often pushes the desire to explore the world to the back burner.

Therefore, we are setting our dreams aside, giving our responsibilities and problems priority over our happiness and mental wellness. To prioritize travel, one must cultivate a mindset where travel is not a luxury, but a necessary component for our well-being.

This new viewpoint entails reorganizing what we think we need in life, elevating the experience of learning and global awareness to the same level as job success and financial security. It means saving - money, of course, but also time and effort - to make room in our lives for upcoming journeys.

To make travel a priority involves action. Sign up for travel newsletters, put in place alerts for flight promotions, or become part of communities that exchange travel advice and possibilities.

Keep your travel aspirations close with visual and tangible reminders, whether that's a vision board displaying photos of places you want to visit or a jar collecting every spare coin for your 'Travel Fund.' You need to believe that your adventure will become a reality.

Travel shouldn't be seen as a distant light at the end of the tunnel, a prize you plan to give yourself 'one day,' 'when there's time,' 'when the kids move out', or 'upon retirement.'

By making travel a priority now, you invite the diverse places and cultures of the world to shape and enhance your personal story, adding endless liveliness to your life.

Planning Your Travels Early: Setting the Stage for Your Adventure

To set out on a trip to places you've longed to explore takes more than just excitement; it demands thorough preparation. Organizing your travels ahead of time isn't just advisable; it's a fundamental step toward a hassle-free holiday. This strategy not only helps you find better deals and more options, but also sets the stage for a richer travel experience.

In the professional realm, early notification of your travel plans is critical. Reach out to your employer and discuss your intended absence as soon as you set your dates, ensuring there's ample time to arrange coverage or delegate responsibilities during your time away.

This kind of open communication maintains a positive work atmosphere and grants you peace of mind. You can take your break with confidence, as you have ensured that things at work are taken care of.

Keep in mind, thorough planning is a traveler's trusted ally. It will be the difference between a decent holiday and a remarkable adventure.

By arranging everything well before you leave, you're not just organizing a journey; you're crafting an unforgettable experience that's customized to your taste and free from the unnecessary setbacks that often accompany last-minute plans. Of course, remember to leave time for spontaneity. No itinerary is set in stone, always allow room for change.

CHAPTER 3

Navigating Language Differences

Unlocking Worldly Adventures

One substantial obstacle that often discourages individuals from exploring different countries is the challenge of language differences.

The overwhelming thought of not being able to communicate, especially in urgent scenarios like emergencies or basic navigating needs, often keeps people tied to the comfort of their native countries. Some worries that may haunt them: "What if I require assistance? What if I get lost? What if I need medical help?"

As a seasoned traveler, I can assure you, these worries, while valid, should not be the walls that confine your spirit of adventure. I've wandered through the art-rich streets of France and delighted in Italy's gastronomic treasures, without speaking French or Italian.

Indeed, I equipped myself with key phrases, but being fluent was far from it. Was I apprehensive? Certainly. But did it disrupt my voyage or diminish the pleasure of discovery? Not in the slightest. I was able to manage, and survived, without speaking the local language.

Nowadays, advances in technology are erasing these language boundaries. Many translation apps can transform your mobile device into a personal translator, something that has proved essential during my journeys.

These electronic aids assist not just in ordinary conversation but also allow you to dive deeper into local languages, often enriching social encounters and understanding of cultural complexities.

The decisive point, however, lies in our attitude. If we regard language barriers as unbeatable obstacles, we rob ourselves of experiencing the world's diversity. If we see them as minor bumps along the road, we learn to navigate, accept them, and enjoy the voyage.

These adventures shape our global insight and nurture a special self-reliance and adaptability that we might not have known we were capable of.

Thus, we shouldn't allow the uneasiness of unknown languages to overshadow our sense of wonder. The world is a vibrant mixture of societies, and our engagements, whether through broken sentences or mutual smiles, integrate us into this world.

Welcome the unfamiliar, as it makes up the very essence of exploration.

CHAPTER 4

Safety Concerns

A Prudent Approach to Travel Safety

S afety is essential, a fact that remains constant, whether we are in the sanctuary of our homes or journeying through different countries.

The idea of venturing into unknown countries often comes with unease, many times intensified by the unknown aspects of these distant places or misinformation.

Yet, these safety worries, while legitimate, should not act as barriers that dampen your desire to travel, especially when the destination has been a long-time dream. In our current era, dangers can hide anywhere, even in our front yard, rendering safety somewhat subjective.

However, it's true that specific destinations need a greater level of caution. The solution? Thorough investigation.

Prior to setting off on any expedition, especially overseas, it's crucial to study the safety dynamics of your intended destination. This involves going beyond a simple online inquiry; it means consulting reliable sources, including federal travel advisories and safety briefs.

Understand the landscape, both geographical and political, and familiarize yourself with local customs that might influence your safety.

Travel insurance, though often overlooked, serves as your quiet protector. Although it might seem like an unnecessary cost, it's as vital as any other travel requirement.

Just as health insurance protects against unexpected health costs, travel insurance acts as a financial buffer, protecting you from unexpected expenses related to travel disruptions or urgent situations.

I undertake my own global explorations, recognizing the associated risks. Accepting the potential for unexpected circumstances and being cautious. This consciousness doesn't diminish the joy of my travels; on the contrary, it enables me to travel more wisely and with greater assurance.

Remember, letting fears dictate your decisions gives them unwarranted power. Instead, arm yourself with information, safeguard your journey with insurance, and embrace the adventure that awaits.

Life, in all its unpredictability, is to be lived to the fullest—explore, discover, and celebrate the experiences your travels bring!

CHAPTER 5
Charting Family Voyages
Mastering the Art of Travel with Children

Traveling with children can be a rewarding and enriching experience, but it's no secret that it comes with many challenges. From the endless packing of diapers and toys, to managing sleep schedules, and keeping little ones entertained during long journeys. The prospect of family travel can sometimes feel overwhelming and, many times, inconceivable.

These difficulties, intense as they are, should not dissuade you from pursuing these rich experiences with your offspring. These inconveniences are critical components of the voyage, serving as channels for invaluable teachings and the formation of unforgettable memories.

A prevalent difficulty for parents is the disruptions of established routines. Children flourish in consistency, and the erratic nature of travels could disturb the structure they are used to. While this may lead to tantrums or sleepless nights, it's an opportunity for them to adapt to new situations and environments, which fosters resilience and flexibility.

Think of it as the body's process of acquiring antibodies. If you don't expose your body to pathogens, it cannot generate the antibodies it will need to fight against diseases.

Hence, it is important for children to be exposed to traveling and all the difficulties it entails. They will learn and adapt. The more often children are exposed to it, the easier it will get every time.

The packing process may feel like a never-ending puzzle, with suitcases bursting at the seams with baby gear, strollers, toys, and snacks. It's true that traveling light becomes a distant memory when kids are in tow.

However, the upside is that you learn to prioritize the essentials and embrace a minimalist mindset. Over time, you'll become a packing pro, and the joy of exploring unknown places will far outweigh the packing troubles.

Navigating unfamiliar environments can be another challenge, but it's also an opportunity for growth and bonding. Children learn problem-solving skills as they adapt to new surroundings, and you'll witness their sense of wonder as they discover the world's treasures, whether it's a colorful market in Marrakech or a pristine beach in Bali.

Your role as a parent becomes that of a guide and mentor, showing them the beauty of the world and nurturing their curiosity.

Yes, traveling with children can and will be demanding, but the experiences and memories you create together are priceless. Don't let the fear of the unknown or the challenges of the journey hold you back.

Embrace the chaos, savor the joy, and remember that family adventures are not just about the destination; they're about the journey and the bonds that grow stronger with each adventure.

So, pack your bags, gather your little ones, and set off on an incredible journey that will shape your family's story for years to come. The world is waiting, and your children are ready to explore it with you.

CHAPTER 6

Defining Travel Age

Your Passport Knows No Age

Is there such a thing as being too old to travel? The very notion is a misconception we're here to debunk. Travel isn't a privilege reserved for the young, but a joyous journey accessible to anyone with the spirit for adventure.

If you are mobile, with or without help, and free from prohibitive medical restrictions, the world remains an open book, waiting for you to turn its pages.

The concept of age is self-imposed, a barrier erected by societal expectations rather than any real limitations. There's profound truth in the motto, "You're only as young as you feel." This belief isn't about denying the realities of aging, but about embracing the passion for life that knows no chronological bounds.

Certainly, aging bodies demand consideration and care, and perhaps our travel adventures might differ from those of our youth, and there's nothing wrong with that.

Some activities could be challenging, but how will you recognize your limits if you don't venture out and test them? How will you know you don't enjoy zip lining or snorkeling until you try it? It is like trying new food, you won't know if you like it until you taste it.

Someone displayed this principle during a cave-exploration tour I took in Mexico. Amongst a group of younger participants was a lady in her early seventies. I had to learn her age, so I asked.

She crawled through small spaces, tackled challenging rocks, and swam in a subterranean river. Though, assisted by a cane, her spirit and determination overshadowed any physical aid.

Her resilience was a testament, inspiring everyone, including myself. She didn't "manage" to complete the course; she thrived; she embraced every moment of the adventure without a hint of complaint.

Her courage wasn't just in participating; it was in casting aside any societal expectations of what aging individuals "should" or "shouldn't" do. This lady helped me realize that there's nothing I can't do if I put my mind and effort into it.

Her experience serves me as a powerful reminder: age isn't a limitation. It's a collection of experiences, wisdom, and a developing capacity for adventure. It underscores that our vitality is not determined by the years we've marked in our calendar but by the depth of experiences we continue to pursue.

So, cast aside the numbers, the "shoulds," "laters", "too tired", and the "too lates." Let's look beyond age, societal expectations, and the barriers we often place on ourselves.

If you feel the call, don't limit yourself. Engage in travel with a timeless passion, understanding that it's less about distance covered and more about the richness of experiences.

When we scrutinize these travel myths, they reveal themselves for what they are—baseless perceptions. These are self-imposed constraints and unfounded fears that chain our adventurous spirit.

Whether deterred by concerns about age, language proficiency, safety, or time, solutions await those who seek them.

Travel isn't a club exclusive to the young, those who speak many languages, or the fearless; it's a big, exciting picture that's ready for anyone who wants to join in. By debunking these notions, we liberate ourselves from reservations and uncertainties, making way for endless possibilities.

So, pack your bags, toss out the doubts, and remember: the horizon is just a journey away. Now, as we embark into the next chapter, we explore something even more exciting—the undeniable benefits of traveling.

Remember, traveling isn't just about collecting stamps in a passport or pictures for social media. This journey is about travel's transformative essence—how it reshapes our worldviews, expands our horizons, and rejuvenates our spirit.

Ready to explore why taking that trip is about more than escaping life but embracing it? Join me as we navigate this illuminating voyage.

The Rewards of Traveling
Understanding the Benefits of Travel

In today's fast-paced world, travel serves as an antidote to the limitations often brought about by our personal and professional routines. It's not just a break from the daily grind; it's a path to personal growth, understanding, and renewal.

As we embark on this section, we explore the comprehensive benefits of traveling, digging into its profound impact not just as a leisure activity, but as a promoter for improvement in our physical, mental, and emotional well-being.

First, we'll navigate through the realm of mental wellness, we'll explore how travel acts as a reset button for our minds. Beyond mere relaxation and stress-reduction, travel exposes us to diverse environments, sharpening our adaptability and sparking creativity.

Overcoming travel challenges boosts problem-solving skills and resilience, while engagement in different settings fosters self-examination and personal growth.

Next, we turn to the physical advantages of being on the move. Whether it's wandering through a new city, hiking unfamiliar terrains, or taking part in local activities, these physical engagements often surpass our regular exertion levels, promoting cardiovascular health and even strengthening our immunity.

We'll also examine the social and emotional perks of travel. The bonds formed on the road, the camaraderie with individuals from varying backgrounds, and the deepened understanding of how diverse cultures enrich our emotional lives.

These interactions enhance our interpersonal skills, push our boundaries beyond our comfort zone, and often lead to friendships that add a new depth to our lives.

We'll investigate how travel broadens our perspectives, encouraging a global mindset. Exposure to new cultures, customs, and histories challenges preconceived notions, leading to a more open, accepting worldview.

As we journey through this exploration, it becomes clear that travel is no mere luxury; it is a necessary endeavor for anyone seeking a fuller, more connected experience of life.

Each trip, no matter how small, peels back the layers of our understanding, revealing more of the world — and ourselves — than we knew before.

Before digging into the various benefits of travel, it's important to note that I am not a health professional, and the insights shared in these chapters are based on personal experiences and observations.

Traveling has had a profound impact on my well-being and perspective, and it's crucial to understand that individual experiences can vary.

What has been transformative for me may not hold the same effect for everyone, as we all interact with environments and respond to experiences differently. Therefore, while I share what travel has offered me, hoping to inspire you, these reflections are not one-size-fits-all recommendations.

Always consider your personal circumstances, consult with health professionals when necessary, and approach any travel-related changes to your lifestyle with mindfulness and caution. So, pack light and carry an open mind; the greatest journey is just ahead.

CHAPTER 7

Mental Health

Navigating the Connection Between Exploration and Mental Wellness

We've examined various misconceptions and barriers associated with travel, recognizing that while these concerns are legitimate, they're not unbeatable.

Now, we shift our focus to the substantial benefits of travel, which are several and significant, especially concerning mental wellness. Let's consider some of these key benefits.

Travel's Effects on Stress Relief

Statistics

In modern society, stress is a predominant issue, often worsened by the multitude of professional and personal responsibilities individuals juggle daily. Excessive stress, if unmanaged, can manifest physically and psychologically, resulting in symptoms like anxiety, muscle tension, fatigue, lack of focus, and impaired memory.

Several studies underline the relationship between travel and stress reduction. A notable study from August 2005 by the National Library of Medicine and the National Center for Biotechnology Information[1] highlighted that women who vacation less frequently, once every two years, showed higher susceptibility to depression and stress than those vacationing multiple times a year.

Further, a December 2013 report from the Transamerica Center for Retirement Studies and the Global Coalition on Aging[2] showed that 78% of respondents experienced decreased stress levels through travel. Remarkably, 87% of active travelers aged 40-49 attributed travel to enhanced long-term health and wellness.

The American Institute of Stress's CompPshyc StressPulse Report[3] revealed alarming levels of workplace stress, with 62% of surveyed North American employees experiencing significant stress, leading to feelings of exhaustion and a sense of losing control.

Travel has emerged as a beneficial intervention, offering a break from daily pressures, and contributing to lowered cortisol levels, inducing a state of calm and contentment. Cortisol, a crucial steroid hormone, aids in responding to stress and various essential physiological processes.

Stress Reduction

Embarking on a travel journey offers a remarkable chance for travelers to disengage from the constant demands of their everyday lives. The very act of leaving behind the familiar, from work pressures to social and family obligations, signals the mind to enter a different mode.

---

1. Chikani, V., Reding, D., Gunderson, P., & McCarty, C. A. (2005). *Vacations improve mental health among rural women: the Wisconsin Rural Women's Health Study* (Report No. 104(6):20-3). National Library of Medicine. https://pubmed.ncbi.nlm.nih.gov/16218311/

2. *Journey to Healthy Aging: Planning for Travel in Retirement* (2013). Transamerica Center for Retirement Studies, Global Coalition on Aging. https://transamericacenter.org/retirement-research/travel-survey

3. *CompPsych StressPulse Report* (2013). ComPsych Corporation. https://www.stress.org/workplace-stress

Immersing oneself in new landscapes, cultures, and activities facilitates a mental and emotional shift, interrupting the usual stress response.

As travelers engage with the present moment, whether by admiring a scenic view or tasting exotic cuisines, they often experience a profound sense of contentment and happiness that remains long after they're back home.

Travel serves as a powerful antidote to stress. It gives us a chance to breathe, find joy in the moment, and return home with a refreshed outlook on life. This peaceful impact, gained through our adventures, often lingers, transforming our approach to life's hustle and bustle.

So, as we venture out, we don't just escape stress; we learn to manage it better, carrying the tranquility we find on our travels back into our everyday lives.

No matter how packed my travel schedule might be, or the number of attractions I aim to see, I always find myself at ease and stress-free during my travels. Traveling, an activity that ignites my passion, brings me a sense of peace rather than pressure, regardless of the pace.

It is critical to acknowledge travel as a temporary solution, one part of a comprehensive approach to mental well-being. It is not a comprehensive solution to chronic stress management issues.

For those facing severe stress, travel complements, but doesn't replace expert medical guidance and intervention.

By embracing travel's ability to refresh and revitalize, we can make informed, healthy decisions that benefit us in the short term and contribute to our long-term mental health.

Enhances Creativity

Travel is a promoter for cognitive change, pushing the brain to think in new patterns and to adapt to new stimuli.

As travelers navigate unfamiliar territories, they encounter diverse perspectives, traditions, and ways of life.

These experiences stimulate different areas of the brain, promoting thought processes that differ from the way of thinking that is common in routine environments.

Such active thinking enhances creativity and innovation, qualities that are highly regarded both personally and professionally.

By stepping outside their cultural comfort zone, individuals can gain fresh insights and new ways of approaching challenges, whether in art, business, or personal life.

Builds Resilience & Mental Agility

The unpredictable nature of travel means individuals often face unexpected situations, from language barriers to logistical complications.

These challenges need rapid problem-solving and decision-making under unfamiliar circumstances, enhancing cognitive functioning and emotional control.

Through overcoming travel difficulties, individuals develop a stronger sense of confidence and a greater tolerance for unexpected situations.

This ability to adapt, known as mental agility, is crucial for handling life's unpredictable moments.

Overcoming challenges while traveling equips individuals with resilience, making them better prepared to handle common stressors, and face life's challenges with determination and a calm attitude.

Self-Discovery and Personal Growth

Travel offers a unique chance for self-reflection, away from the distractions of the daily routine. By exploring new countries, individuals not only learn about different cultures but also reflect on their own preconceptions, values, and aspirations.

Being away from the usual distractions helps individuals think about their life's direction and what truly matters to them. The experiences of travel, whether learning something new or overcoming challenges, help in understanding one's strengths and limitations.

For many, travel becomes a journey of personal growth, leading to a clearer sense of purpose and satisfaction.

These points illustrate just a fraction of the mental wellness benefits that travel can offer. It's important to recognize travel not only as a leisure activity but also as a valuable investment in one's mental and emotional health.

Boosting Mental Focus and Productivity Through Exploration

Stress can take a toll on our mental clarity and productivity. When we're constantly immersed in the demands and routines of daily life, our minds can become overwhelmed, leading to reduced concentration and cognitive function.

However, travel offers a powerful antidote to this mental fatigue. By stepping away from the familiar and breaking the daily monotonous cycle, you provide your mind with a much-needed reset.

Travel introduces novelty and excitement into your life, stimulating your senses and encouraging you to be present in the moment, and leave behind the stressors of everyday life.

A recent poll conducted by eDreams ODIGEO[4] between March 14 and 15, 2023, sheds light on the positive impact of travel on mental well-being. The poll surveyed individuals from different regions, with 58% of participants from the Northeast Coast of the United States and 48% of participants in the Midwest reporting that travel had a beneficial effect on their mental well-being.

These findings underline the notion that travel not only provides an escape from stress but also rejuvenates the mind, enhancing mental focus and productivity.

---

4. *eDreams' latest Poll reveals our Motivations for planning Detox Breaks* (2023). One Poll for eDreams ODIGEO. https://www.prnewswire.com/news-releases/edreams-latest-poll-reveals-our-motivations-for-planning-detox-breaks-301931637.html

Enhancing Emotional Health: The Power of Travel

Travel is more than just an action; it's an emotional journey that pierces our mental health. The thrill often starts with the mere thought of a new adventure, be it visiting a new destination, tasting authentic cuisines, or diving into a distinct culture. Just this anticipation can be a significant mood-booster.

Journeying, whether with friends, family or solo, allows us to craft precious lasting memories. Imagine conquering the historic peaks of Machu Picchu, witnessing the panoramic views from atop the Eiffel Tower, or reflecting on the peaceful joy of stepping onto the stunning beaches of Santorini.

These unique experiences forge unforgettable memories that enrich our emotional well-being.

The exposure to stunning, unfamiliar landscapes can invigorate the senses and elevate mood levels, providing a kind of joy that material possessions often can't match.

The prospect of travel can keep us motivated and cheerful, with the positive effects being strong as the departure date draws closer.

Indeed, in this context, one could argue that investing in travel can indeed "buy" happiness, offering a fulfillment that is rarely derived from other forms of spending.

CHAPTER 8

Fortifying the Body

The Road to Robust Health

It is known that prolonged stress can weaken our immune system, leaving us vulnerable to many health problems. However, the antidote might be simpler than we think: taking a genuine break.

Travel isn't just a pause from our daily routine; it's a meaningful breather that revitalizes our body and mind and strengthens our immune defenses.

Exposing ourselves in new environments benefits our immune system. By facing atypical pathogens, the body learns and produces new antibodies, making it more vigilant and prepared.

This natural boost is a lesser-known perk of exploring new locales. Of course, this doesn't mean you can't get sick while traveling, but under normal circumstances, it could boost your immune system.

Travel often means spending more time outdoors interacting with the environment. Prolonged outdoor activity increases exposure to sunlight, essential for Vitamin D synthesis, which plays an important role in immunity, inflammation control, and regulating glucose.

Activities like strolling on a sunny beach or wandering through a new city's streets contribute to our physical wellness.

Physical activity is fundamental to traveling. Sightseeing often involves more walking than we're accustomed to, promoting cardiovascular health through improved circulation and endurance. The culinary aspect of travel encourages healthier eating habits by offering opportunities to indulge in local, fresh produce, often a refreshing change from our fast-food-dominated diets.

After an invigorating day filled with exploration and adventure, what could be more satisfying than a good night's sleep? Travel often remedies sleep irregularities, with physical exhaustion leading to deeper, more restful slumber.

In conclusion, travel isn't a mere indulgence but a large contributor to our physical well-being.

Beyond the immediate pleasure and relaxation it offers, each journey enhances our health in noticeable ways, providing a compelling reason to prioritize and cherish our vacations.

CHAPTER 9

Living in the Moment

A Pause from Digital Overload

In our digitally driven world, travel offers a unique opportunity: the chance to unplug and truly immerse ourselves in the present moment.

Often, the allure of unknown places is so strong that our gadgets take a back seat, replaced by the vivid experiences ready for us to embrace with undivided attention.

Part of the therapeutic power of travel lies in this very disconnection. Stepping away from the ceaseless buzz of notifications, social media posts, and checking emails allows us to engage with our surroundings.

This isn't about observing, but truly seeing—appreciating the beauty of our surroundings. While social media and messages remain a click away, they can wait. They will still be there to capture our stories at the end of the day or, even better, upon our return home.

Think of the peaceful landscapes or bustling city scenes we encounter while traveling. They deserve our full attention. Their magic diminishes if we're constantly interrupted by emails, notifications, or calls.

Personally, I've found a balance by using my phone mainly for taking photos and navigating during my trips, saving chats and social media for quiet times back at my hotel.

Disconnecting also reopens the doors to human connection. Without our eyes glued to screens, we can dive into local life, chat with people, join activities, and create connections that go beyond mere location.

These interactions, unfiltered through digital mediums, are the essence of genuine human connection.

In conclusion, for a richer, more authentic travel experience, we should commit our digital devices to a minimal role.

By doing this, we allow ourselves to fully absorb the world around us, making memories more vivid and personal. It's more than just seeing new places; it's about learning to be truly present.

CHAPTER 10

Embarking on a Journey of Self-Discovery

How Travel Shapes Personal Growth

Every trip we take adds a unique chapter to our life's story. Whether you're an experienced traveler or someone setting out for the first time, every journey promises personal growth. But traveling does more than just fill our passports, it transforms us in deeper ways, right to our core.

Traveling is great for personal growth. It lets us dive into new cultures, see the world in new ways, and expand our perspectives. It puts us in situations that challenge us, helping us to adapt and find strengths we didn't know we had.

By going to unknown places, we learn more about ourselves, our character, and where we are headed in life. Every trip, with its highs and lows, acts like a mirror that shows us our strengths and areas we can improve.

For example, those of us who travel alone experience the true value of being self-sufficient, leaning on our skills, intuition, and resourcefulness.

This kind of independence makes us feel more confident in all areas of life. While we get to know a culture that's different from our own, we develop empathy and a broader understanding — qualities that are important for personal growth and becoming a thoughtful human being.

Thinking about our travels and what we've learned from them, we see how they help shape us. Travel doesn't just show us the world; it lets the world change us, one trip at a time.

Cultural Awareness

Travel lets us see the wide variety of cultures, traditions, and worldviews. It helps us learn about things that differ from what we know and helps us value how people from different backgrounds live and what they believe in.

Think about a world without this variety; it wouldn't be as interesting as the diverse world we live in. It's like a garden's beauty because of its diversity of flowers, each one adding to the complexity and beauty of its landscape.

Empathy and Compassion

Travel takes us out of our comfort zones and shows us what life is like in different places, from busy cities to peaceful countryside villages.

As we move through these different settings, we get to see how other people live their daily lives. We notice the determined looks of city folks navigating the complexities of urban life, and the shared smiles of villagers working in close-knit communities.

The best part of these journeys is often the silent bonds we form with others, which help us forge feelings of empathy and compassion, even if we don't speak the same language or share the same culture.

Whether it's kids playing together outside, kind strangers telling us their stories, or seeing that everyone has struggles and dreams, these experiences foster a heartfelt compassion that lingers long after our return home.

Travel is more than an escape from our routine. It makes us appreciate what we have and encourages us to extend a hand, an ear, a hug, or a smile to those we meet.

In the end, the journey not only teaches us about the world but also makes us more compassionate and caring toward the people in it.

Adaptability

The unpredictable nature of travel is like a learning experience for our minds. It throws many unexpected situations at us that help us learn to adapt.

We must adapt when we miss a flight, and we must figure out what to do next right away. When we need to communicate with people who speak an unfamiliar language or find a place to stay at a moment's notice.

Even though these situations can be stressful for some, they teach us a valuable lesson; that we can get through unforeseen problems, often by using a resourcefulness we never knew we possessed.

These instances of unforeseen challenges do more than just alter our immediate plans; they teach us to be flexible in how we think about the unknown. We learn how there are many ways to get to where we're going and adapt.

The adaptability we get from traveling gives us a strength that we carry into our daily lives. The resourcefulness we uncover in a new country becomes something we rely on back home, giving us the confidence that we can handle whatever life may throw our way.

And as we face these difficulties and get past them, we realize that adapting isn't just about avoiding problems. It's about welcoming change, finding happiness, and learning from it.

Travel teaches us this clever trick: to turn every obstacle into an opportunity, and to come out of each experience not just okay, but better and more flexible than ever before.

Confidence

Every challenge we overcome during our travels, whether it's figuring out public transportation in a new city or bargaining in a local market, boosts our self-confidence.

Travel is about the little and big wins we have along the way, which makes us feel proud in a way that gathering border stamps doesn't.

For example, by pushing ourselves to do things that make us feel uncomfortable, like making ourselves understood despite not knowing the language well, or finding our way in a new city, we build our confidence.

The small wins matter as well—like getting a smile despite a language barrier, successfully getting a taxi in a foreign city, or enjoying a meal with people we've just met on our travels.

It's not just about gathering experiences, but about proving to ourselves that we can adapt and handle different situations.

At the end of a tough hike or after finding your way in a new city, there might not be a certificate or diploma to show for it, but the sense of achievement you will feel is very real. You carry that feeling with you as quiet proof of what you're capable of.

The real treasures of traveling are those quiet moments when we realize we can do more than we thought. These are treasures that far outweigh the mere act of sightseeing. These are the experiences that stay with us, shaping who we are and pushing us to take on even bigger adventures.

Communication Skills

Travel often means communicating across language barriers. When we try to understand and be understood, using gestures, patience, and sometimes humor, it not only makes our trip richer, but also improves our ability to connect with others. Every time we communicate, it proves that connection goes beyond words.

When we try to understand new languages, we get better at noticing the small things in communication. We get good at reading body language, listening for what people mean, and saying what we think in a simple way that focuses on being clear and showing feeling.

The effort of communicating in new and different situations also makes us more empathetic. We become more patient, better listeners, and more creative in trying to understand different ways of talking.

This makes our travels more meaningful and makes us value the many ways we can share thoughts and feelings every day.

In a world where we often talk through phone screens, the real, sometimes tough talks we have while traveling remind us of the human essence at the heart of communication.

Laughing at a joke with street vendor, the satisfaction of successfully asking for directions, the bond formed through helping a fellow traveler — these moments make us realize that our ability to connect is not limited by language. It's endless and comes from being human.

When we come back from our travels, we're more confident in our ability to express ourselves, solve problems, and make friends in all parts of our lives and the world.

Travel shows us that every conversation is a way to connect, and with the right approach, we can cross any gap.

Self-Discovery

Every trip pushes our boundaries. Trying new exotic dishes, joining in on local traditions, or going on exciting adventures also means we're learning about who we are. These experiences, exhilarating, unfamiliar, or even intimidating, help us think about ourselves and grow.

Travel also acts as a propeller for uncovering strengths and vulnerabilities we may not have recognized. It can show us the depths of our courage when we navigate a foreign land solo, or the resilience we keep within when we find our way through a challenging situation.

Even the moments of solitude that travel can sometimes bring are opportunities to talk with our inner selves, to listen to the often-overlooked inner voice that whispers truths about who we are and who we might become.

With every new thing we experience, we learn a little more about our values, beliefs, and what we want in life. Our travels act like a mirror showing us who we are and asking us to think about how we fit into the wider world.

They make us question ourselves: Are we as open-minded as we think? How do we adapt to change? What brings us genuine joy?

Travel isn't just about visiting different locations; it's a journey of personal growth. The things we see and the people we meet shape who we become.

By traveling, we become more open-minded, flexible, confident, with enriched communication skills, and a deepened understanding of ourselves and the world. Every trip, with its unique challenges and rewards, is a step towards becoming a better version of ourselves.

Every journey enriches our life story, offering chances for growth and change.

CHAPTER 11

Traveling Together
Building Bonds Across Boundaries

Traveling together can have a profound impact on bonding and strengthening relationships, whether it's with your partner, family members or friends. Together, you will support each other during any unexpected events, learn from it and even laugh about it later. Here are some ways in which travel fosters stronger bonds:

Creating Memories Together

Every journey comes with its unique experiences and challenges. These moments, whether they are exhilarating or challenging, become shared stories you will look back on and cherish.

Beyond the laughter and snapshots, the shared trials and triumphs encountered on a journey become memories you will all remember. Whether it's the shared relief of finding your way after getting lost or the shared awe at a sunset that colors the sky, these experiences become part of your shared history.

You will recount the stories of how you navigated new territories or braved recent adventures at gatherings, reminding you both of your journey's unique bond and the wealth of memories you've accumulated side by side.

Quality Time

Travel often provides quality time with your loved ones away from distractions and the demands of everyday life. This uninterrupted time will allow space to have deeper conversations and connections.

The time spent together on the road is a precious breather from the ticking clocks of daily routine. It's in these moments, perhaps while waiting for a train or lounging on a beach, that you find the luxury of uninterrupted time to get into meaningful conversations.

Such quality time enriches relationships, building shared experiences and mutual understanding.

Communication and Teamwork

Travel requires talking about travel plans, preferences, and interests, which promotes better understanding and encourages open communication with your travel partner.

Besides communicating, you will be required to work as a team and cooperate with each other to solve unexpected travel challenges.

As you discuss routes and options, listen to each other's preferences, and compromise, your collective voice grows stronger. This dialogue and decision-making not only fine-tunes your communication skills but also highlights the importance of teamwork.

Each successful navigation through the day's itinerary or each problem solved together is a testament to the power of working in unison.

Shared Interests

When you travel, your interests and/or passions often align with those of your travel partner. Whether you share love for art, culture, history, or food, exploring these interests together can strengthen your relationship and bond.

The joy of travel is amplified when you experience it with someone who appreciates the same parts of life that you do.

As you both stand before a masterpiece in a museum, or savor the flavors of a new cuisine, these shared passions become the glue that binds your experiences.

The enthusiasm is contagious, the satisfaction mutual, and it is in these moments that your bond deepens, grounded in a common appreciation for the things that you both love.

Building Trust

Travel can build trust in relationships as you rely on each other for support and navigation. Mutual trust is strengthened when you can count on your travel companion in unfamiliar environments, knowing they will not let you down.

When the map fails, and technology falters, it's the mutual trust you have in one another that becomes your true north.

Each decision to trust your partner's instincts or to share the responsibility in an unfamiliar place strengthens the trust that is foundational to any strong relationship. It's the assurance that you have each other's backs, the unspoken pact of support and reliability.

Rekindles Romance

Last, but not least, travel can help you rekindle romance with your partner. Turn on the flame that might have been extinguishing.

By spending quality time together, without the usual stressors of your daily routine, you will concentrate on enjoying your time together. Hence, aiding the rediscovery of that romantic connection.

The excitement you experience while doing new things together and exploring unknown places can bring back the spark that daily routines might have dimmed.

Every time you look at each other while seeing something new, dance together in the rain, or choose to be with each other instead of doing anything else, it's like adding fuel to a fire, making the warm feelings and closeness between you stronger. Hence, renewing intimacy and affection.

In conclusion, travel is far more than a journey between geographical locations. It's a gateway to closer, stronger relationships forged in the shared adventures, challenges, and triumphs that travel entails.

These journeys compel us to reconnect, not just with the world, but with those beside us, offering a unique space where relationships can flourish, unrestricted by the routine of daily life.

CHAPTER 12

Embracing the World

A Journey into Cultural Appreciation Through Travel

Travel opens our eyes and hearts to the vast diversity of our world. It allows us to step beyond our own cultural norms and immerse ourselves in the beauty and complexity of different ways of life. Let's talk about how traveling can make us value cultural diversity:

Celebrating Differences

Travel is a celebration of the world's varied cultural spectrum. It shifts our perspective from judgment to acknowledgment, turning cultural differences from barriers into points of interest, admiration, and respect.

Promoting Peace Through Understanding

Travel does more than just help us appreciate other cultures; it helps spread peace, tolerance, and love. By dismissing ignorance and discrediting stereotypes, we foster mutual understanding. Nurturing a world where diversity is our strength, not a pretext for discrimination.

Travel is more than just a trip—it's a way to learn, grow, respect, and appreciate the many cultures around us. It not only enriches our lives, but also fosters a deeper understanding of our shared humanity.

CHAPTER 13

Exploring Career Paths Through Travel

Discovering Work and Business Possibilities on the Go

Travel isn't just about exploring unknown places; it's also a gateway to opportunities that can change your work life and financial future. When you travel, you're doing more than just taking a break from the usual; you're stepping into a world where new career and money-making opportunities are waiting.

In this last section, we'll inspect how every trip can be a steppingstone for your career growth and financial prospects. It's all about seeing every journey as a school where you learn the secrets of working and winning in the worldwide marketplace.

Networking

In your travels, each new acquaintance has the potential to enrich your life. The chances are that encounters at a hostel common room, the shared taxi rides, or the conversations struck up over a street food stall can unravel into significant networking opportunities.

The people you meet while traveling may become your future business partners, mentors, collaborators, or new friends. Each exchange is an opportunity to share ideas and dreams, and these can very often lay the groundwork for future professional ventures or strengthen your social circle with the addition of global friendships.

Language Skills

Traveling to foreign countries can improve your language skills, which could be an asset in the global job market. Bilingual or multilingual individuals are often in high demand, especially in industries with international reach.

When you're navigating a market's noise or asking for directions in a foreign tongue, every attempt at communication improves your language skills. This linguistic ability can make you stand out in an interconnected world where cultural fluency is valued.

Learning a new language can provide cognitive benefits such as improving memory, learning, brain function, problem-solving capabilities, multi-tasking skills, and protects the brain against the natural decline of cognitive functions, among other benefits.[1] These are all traits that could help make any professional more adaptable and effective.

But beyond the useful, the act of learning a language is an exercise in cultural respect—it's a gesture that says, 'I value your culture enough to learn your language.' It equips you with not just a new way to converse, but a new way to think, opening doors to cultural empathy.

Inspiration and Creativity

Travel can inspire new ideas and perspectives, which can be beneficial for careers in creative fields such as writing, art, design, technology, and innovation.

---

1. Marian, V. Ph.D., Shook, A. (2012). *The Cognitive Benefits of Being Bilingual.* (PMID: 23447799). National Library of Medicine. https://www.ncbi.nlm.nih.gov/pmc/articles/PMC3583091/

These experiences feed the imagination, pushing the boundaries of conventional thought. For the artist, the writer, the entrepreneur, or the designer, travel can act as an inspiration, igniting the spark of creation.

Business Opportunities

With every land you navigate, you become more attuned to the patterns of different markets and consumer cultures. This awareness can be the seed of a flourishing business idea or a strategic partnership.

For the observant traveler, every cultural distinction or economic pattern can spell opportunity—a chance to bridge markets, to innovate, to introduce a product or service that speaks to a need or desire you've seen echoed in the streets and stories of people miles away from home.

Market Research

Your travel adventures can also serve as market research, by allowing you to gain insight into consumer preferences and market trends in different countries. This information can be valuable for entrepreneurs and business professionals.

Your journeys allow you to witness firsthand the flow of commerce across cultures. Observing the locals' preferences in fashion, technology, or food can offer invaluable insights that transcend any data a report could provide.

For the astute entrepreneur or business strategist, these observations are data points, informing a global perspective that can predict trends, inspire new product lines, or suggest new marketing strategies.

Building your Personal Brand

Sharing your travel experiences on social media or through a blog can enhance your personal brand. It could position you as an expert in travel-related fields, leading to opportunities such as sponsored travel, travel writing, or photography.

This narrative can be a beacon to others who aspire to similar paths, setting you apart as a leader in travel thought and experiences.

Your stories become your brand, and in this digital age, this brand is currency. It can open doors to ambassadorships, speaking engagements, and other professional opportunities that value worldly experience and the ability to communicate to a public.

In conclusion, travel embodies a great number of opportunities. It's an enabler not only for personal growth but also for career enhancement and entrepreneurial aspirations.

The world is a classroom, offering lessons through its diverse cultures, languages, and landscapes. When we embark on each journey, we unravel potential networking prospects, business ideas, and avenues for self-promotion and branding that the limitations of our comfort zones could never provide.

This section has illuminated how travel isn't a pause from our professional life but an enriching component of our career journey.

So, pack your suitcases with curiosity and dreams, for every ticket bought opens the door to not just scenic vistas but a horizon of opportunities.

Final Thoughts

On the journey through these pages, we've ventured together across various terrains, from the personal transformations afforded by travel to the bridges it builds between cultures, and the surprising career and economic doors it can open.

Travel, as we've seen, is a comprehensive educator and a facilitator for growth that infuses every aspect of our lives.

This book has shared stories and insights to highlight travel's role in enriching our lives. It's about stepping out of our comfort zone, experiencing the world's diversity, and coming back with greater knowledge, ideas, compassion, and understanding. The world molds us as much as we add to its story.

However, as we conclude this book, it's not the end, but a starting point for your own adventures. Every time you add a new stamp to your passport, you're not just recording visits but broadening your perspective, testing your views, and growing as an informed individual.

As you close this book, think of it as a boarding pass to a journey yet to come. Adventures shaped by your eagerness to learn, and destinations defined by your willingness to embrace life's richness.

Your next adventure is out there, waiting to educate, heal, challenge, and uplift you. Don't procrastinate your journey for 'later', 'when I have time', 'when my boss lets me', or 'when I have the money'. There will always be an impediment to start your adventure.

Break any barrier that is blocking you from starting your travel journey. No impediment is insurmountable. We can overcome all excuses. So, here's to all your future travels—may they be as vast as your desire to discover. Life is only one, don't just survive it. LIVE IT!

Join Our Exclusive Travel Community!

Embark on a Journey with Our Exclusive Travel Community!

Are you ready to elevate your travel experiences? I warmly invite you to join our Travel Readers Club, an exclusive community for those who share a passion for exploration and discovery. As a member, you'll unlock a world of invaluable resources designed to enhance every aspect of your journey.

Imagine having access to the best discounts on airfare and hotels, making your dream destinations more attainable than ever. We'll also provide you with comprehensive packing lists tailored for every season and destination - be it a winter wonderland, a summer beach escape, European adventures, or luxurious cruises.

But that's not all! You'll also discover a suite of essential apps and websites, meticulously curated to help you organize your itineraries, breeze through airport security, and stay informed and safe wherever your travels take you.

Join our Travel Readers Club today and transform the way you travel, making each trip more efficient, enjoyable, and extraordinary. Once you sign up, you will receive a link where you can download the documents containing the above travel resources, and stay updated on new book releases.

Sign up here https://www.rainbowtextpublishing.com/travel-readers-group

All icons are clickable

AIRFARE
Websites/Apps where you can find cheap airfare

TRAVEL APPS

RESOURCES
Resources to help make your travel easier, faster and safe

HOTEL DISCOUNT MEMBERSHIPS

Discounts in airfare and hotels through a membership

If you need help planning that long-awaited adventure, feel free to visit my Travel Agency's, Never Stop Packing Travel, at our website www.NeverStopPacking.com

New Book Coming Soon!

Wander More, Worry Less:
Unlocking the World with Tips, Tricks, and Travel Hacks

Embark on your next journey with confidence and curiosity! Our upcoming book, "Wander More, Worry Less," is your golden ticket to becoming a savvy globetrotter. Filled with ingenious tips, practical tricks, and clever hacks, this guide is crafted to transform your travel experiences.

Whether you're dreaming of exotic beaches, thrilling adventures, or cultural escapades, our book is packed with insider knowledge that will help you navigate the globe like a pro.

Say goodbye to travel stress and hello to unforgettable adventures. Keep an eye out for "Wander More, Worry Less" – your essential companion for smarter, safer, and more joyful journeys!

Turn the page for a brief sneak peek into this exciting new book.

Wander More, Worry Less:

Unlocking the World with Tips, Tricks, and Travel Hacks

W elcome to your next adventure!

Embarking on a journey, whether it's a weekend getaway or a globe-trotting expedition, is an exhilarating experience. But let's face it, the process of planning and traveling can be filled with complexities and unexpected challenges. That's where this book comes in – your ultimate companion to make every trip not just memorable, but also remarkably smooth and affordable.

In these pages, you'll find a treasure trove of tips and tricks that I've meticulously gathered from my own experiences and from seasoned travelers around the world, as well as extensive research. This is not just another travel guide; it's a comprehensive toolkit designed to empower you at every step of your journey.

We'll dive deep into the art of snagging the best deals on airfare and hotels, ensuring that your dream vacation doesn't turn into a financial nightmare. You'll discover a curated list of apps that are not just helpful, but transformative for your travel experience. From speeding through airport security with ease to traveling safely in unknown territories, we've got you covered.

But that's just the beginning. Have you ever found yourself struggling with overpacked luggage or lost in a foreign city? Worry no more! Our practical luggage and packing tips, along with insightful guidance on navigation, will turn you into a savvy traveler in no time.

Budgeting and planning might seem tedious, but with our straightforward and effective strategies, you'll find joy in crafting your perfect itinerary without breaking the bank. We'll also explore the world of travel gadgets – those ingenious inventions that can make a world of difference in your travels.

And because we want you to be a well-informed traveler, we'll shed light on common travel scams and how to avoid them. Plus, there's more – insights on local transportation, food, and unique experiences that await you in different corners of the world.

This book is your passport to traveling smarter, safer, and more enjoyably.

So, pack your bags and let's embark on this journey together. The world is vast and full of wonders, and with this book in hand, you're well-equipped to explore it in ways you never thought possible. Let the adventure begin!

About the Author

Elizabeth Delgado is a multifaceted author who brings a world of experience to her writing. Fully bilingual in English and Spanish, she holds a Bachelor's Degree from EDP University in Puerto Rico, where she spent the formative years of her life.

With a foot in two worlds, Elizabeth bridges the gap between cultures in her lively non-fiction. Elizabeth's academic background infuses her work with precision, clarity and brings a logical yet creative approach to her writing.

Her Puerto Rican roots and current New York City lifestyle provide a vibrant backdrop for her work as a travel agent and author. By day, Elizabeth thrives as a professional in the finance industry in the heart of New York City; by night she operates her home-based travel agency, drawing on her extensive travels to inspire fellow wanderlust seekers.

She's turned her passion for travel into a resource for fellow explorers. Elizabeth's writing not only educates but also inspires readers to discover the joy of travel.

Elizabeth's literary journey doesn't stop at travel; her writing also ventures into subjects close to her heart, reflecting her multifaceted interests and experiences. From the intricacies of daily life to the broader human experience, her words strive to explore and resonate with the nuanced tapestry of human emotions and adventures, inviting readers not only to explore the world beyond but also the universe within.

Keep up with Elizabeth's literary and travel escapades on Facebook @RainbowTextPublishing, or explore her offerings at www.rainbowtextpublishing.com.

Readers and travelers alike are welcome to reach out via email at liz@rainbowtextpublishing.com for any inquiries or travel advice.

Printed in the USA
CPSIA information can be obtained
at www.ICGtesting.com
CBHW070319030724
11009CB00019B/1346